Contents

4   A Word from Nancy

9   Instruments of Grace

35   Making It Personal

39   100 Different Kinds of Kindness

55   Notes

A WORD FROM NANCY

You don't have to look very far to see that there's a crisis of kindness in our world today. Or, to be more accurate, a crisis of a *lack* of kindness.

Incivility, rudeness, and arrogance are the currency of choice in the marketplace of ideas. Dogmatic rants and angry debates are sure to increase ratings on cable and network news channels. On social media, we add filters to disguise blemishes, smooth wrinkles, or to make it look like we're working from the beach, but the internal filter meant to restrain our tongue and behaviors? That one, we leave behind.

And that's just the crisis *outside* of the home. Inside the home, we're not much better. (Sometimes worse!) We're quick to lash out at our families, our words brim with sarcasm, and instead of looking for ways to serve our nearest neighbors, we are intent on promoting *our* comfort, *our* convenience, *our* plans, *our* wishes.

We may know our Bibles well and be able to recite lots of verses. We may affirm what Scripture teaches from cover to cover. But it's not enough to simply have sound doctrine and firm convictions about biblical truth. We also need to be clothed in kindness as we live out that truth and share it with others.

We often think of kindness as an attitude, a spirit, a manner of speaking or being—and it is all of that. But biblical kindness also involves actions and behavior. In fact, elsewhere in Scripture, the word translated "kindness" in Titus 2 is sometimes translated "good." It means to be "benevolent, profitable, useful." It means to be "good in character and beneficial in effect."

You see, Christian kindness is not just a matter of *feeling* kind or *thinking* kind thoughts. It's not just a demeanor that is quiet and non-hostile. It may encompass all of those things, but true kindness is *active* goodness. It's actively influencing others.

During His ministry here on earth, Jesus showed us the heart of His heavenly Father who is kind, compassionate, and does good to His creatures. And astonishingly, God's kindness is not based on the goodness or worthiness of the recipient. This is the standard as we seek to show active kindness—God's kindness—to those around us.

Why does kindness matter so much? What's at stake if we don't live this way? Titus 2:5 reminds us that the purpose is "that the word of God may not be reviled." If we don't live a life of active kindness, people will scoff at the Word of God!

But when we are kind, when we go about doing good—including to those who are ungrateful and undeserving—we stand out. We're countercultural. And most important, we demonstrate the presence of Jesus in our lives when we're different from the self-centered, angry, unkind world around us.

Whether you're older or younger, at work or at home, raising children or serving in the church, I pray this booklet will help you to weave a deeper kind of kindness into the fabric of your life. When we take the deep work of kindness seriously, our enemies "may be put to shame, having nothing evil to say about us" (Titus 2:8). And above all, we will shine a spotlight on Jesus, making the redemption story visible to those who need to hear it, "that in everything [we] may adorn the doctrine of God our Savior" (v. 10).

What a calling! What a responsibility! What a privilege is ours.

~ Nancy DeMoss Wolgemuth

Pure kindness flows from God's saving grace and colors our lives with a joy that is winsomely contagious.

MARY BEEKE

Older women likewise are to be reverent in behavior,
not slanderers or slaves to much wine.
They are to teach what is good,
and so train the young women
to love their husbands and children,
to be self-controlled, pure, working at home,

kind,

and submissive to their own husbands,
that the word of God may not be reviled.

TITUS 2:3–5

INSTRUMENTS OF GRACE

FROM THE LOOK ON WOMEN'S FACES whenever I point them to the vision of mature, Christian womanhood found in Titus 2, it seems many of them care about this ideal. They respect and desire the kind of character God's Word calls them to pursue, and they are intrigued by the possibilities of what God could accomplish in and through their lives if they were to establish the kinds of intergenerational friendships Paul describes in this passage.

Our hearts are drawn to this portrait of a godly woman, the principles she embodies, and what she does to adorn the gospel. But God is not only interested in what we do. He is equally concerned with how we do what we do—with the heart behind our actions.

That's why I believe Paul included an admonition about being *kind* right in the middle of his core curriculum for women in the church (Titus 2:5). In fact, "kind" falls right on the heels of "working at home"—it's included in the context of our most intimate family relationships. The Scripture is saying it's not enough to tend to the tasks and people assigned to us. God also cares about our motives and our disposition—how that service is carried out, how we treat and respond to our family, friends, and others.

Paul is the one, remember, who famously wrote, "If I speak in the tongues of men and of angels . . . if I have prophetic powers, and understand all mysteries and all knowledge . . . if I give away all I have, and if I deliver up my body to be burned, but have not love, I gain nothing" (1 Cor. 13:1–3).

Nothing.

He might similarly say, of women who serve their families and care for their homes, "If I have a house so spotless that people could eat off the kitchen floor . . . and if I can whip up incredibly scrumptious meals on a tight budget . . . and if I've transformed our home into a magazine quality showcase . . . but I don't do it all with kindness, it's nothing."

Because, yes, Jesus can be seen and worshiped through such ordinary things as a crisply ironed dress shirt, a made bed, a ride to soccer practice, even a fresh batch of chocolate-chip cookies.

But not when they're performed without kindness.

Without that quality, those "good" things we do for others amount to noisy gongs and clanging cymbals. (Paul's words again.) And nobody can hear or feel our love for them over the tired, exasperated, frustrated racket we're making.

Like Jesus' friend Martha, we are sometimes "distracted with much serving" (Luke 10:40), "worried and bothered about so many things" (v. 41 NASB). We become stretched thin and stirred up, bothered and brittle.

And, all too often, unkind.

But I think there's often something more than just stress behind the sharp tone or impatient attitude that sometimes bubbles up and spills over as unkindness in our relationships—the lack of a "sound mind."

A self-controlled—*sophron*—mind.

Sophron comes from two other Greek words—*soos,* meaning either "sound" or "saved," and *phren,* meaning "outlook" or "mind." When we put the two together, it means to have a "sound mind" or a "saved mind."

A *sophron* lifestyle begins with a *sophron* state of mind—a way of thinking that affects everything about the way we live. A sensible, sound, self-controlled mindset will result in sensible, sound, self-controlled behavior.

By the same token, irrational, impulsive, undisciplined, out-of-control behavior is evidence of thinking that is not *sophron*.

Because when we're not *sophron,* we're apt to see only what frustrates us, so we begin to resent the very people God has called us to serve.

When we're not *sophron,* we let ourselves get overwhelmed by our schedules and agendas rather than concentrating on the "one thing" Jesus said was "necessary" (Luke 10:42)— experiencing life in His presence.

When we're not *sophron,* we don't have any margin or heart for kindness.

So why don't we just pull over here for a while and drop in on Martha at her home in Bethany. Let's see what the lack of *sophron* did to one woman's mind in particular.

A TALE OF TWO SISTERS

The occasion, you may recall, was a visit by Jesus and a band of His followers. (You can read the whole story in Luke 10.) We don't know for sure how many people were with Him, but it was probably a good-sized traveling party, perhaps two or three dozen people. And Martha, with her take-charge, firstborn temperament, was the de facto hostess for this impromptu gathering.[1]

At first, we assume, Martha was excited to see Jesus and the others in the doorway, thankful for the privilege of hosting her friend in the home she shared with her sister (Mary) and brother (Lazarus). But as Martha scrambled to clean and cook and make sure everyone was properly served and comfortably settled (while Mary chose to sit at Jesus' feet and listen to Him teach), a host of turbulent thoughts and attitudes began swirling in her head and heart.

I'm sure, like me, you'll recognize some of them:

- *Self-centeredness.* "Lord, do you not care that my sister has left me to serve alone? Tell her then to help me" (v. 40). Notice all the first-person language in these biting words, all the concern about "me"—what this responsibility is costing me, what people should be doing for me.

- *Insensitivity.* People had gathered around to listen to Jesus teach. But that didn't keep Martha from barging in, interrupting Him, disturbing everyone. She was more concerned about how she was being inconvenienced than about what others were needing or experiencing.

- *Accusation.* Asking if someone could give her a hand would have been an understandable request. But her words were accusatory—both toward Jesus ("do you not care?") and toward her sister ("my sister has left me to serve alone").

- *Resentment.* We can guess that Martha may have already been clattering the dishes in the kitchen a little more loudly than necessary. Her inner martyr had likely been muttering under her breath for quite a while. And when no one picked up on her "hint, hint" clues, she stopped even trying to squelch her rising anger. Out it came—loud and whiny and, yes, unkind.

Martha had grown irritated, impatient, demanding. There was an edge in her spirit, harshness in her voice. Serving was no longer a privilege—lovingly, gladly, graciously given—but a burden. The friends she had set out to serve had become to her a bother, a nuisance.

And beyond just being selfishly upset, Martha was willing to risk building a wall between herself and her sister. If not for Jesus' wise, gentle, corrective rebuke, we could easily imagine a few subsequent days of...

"Is something wrong, Martha?"

"Nothing's wrong."

"Well, something's wrong. I can tell."

"No, Mary. It's not!"

"Well, it sure seems like it."

"Would you please just stop?"

"Oh, Martha, don't tell me you're still—"

"I don't want to talk about it anymore, okay?"

"It was just that Jesus was here, and—"

"Exactly! And I would have been fine if you'd ..."

The Scripture doesn't tell us what took place between the sisters after Jesus' visit. But when *sophron*—a sound mind, self-controlled thinking—goes missing, unkindness all-too-often shows up in its place, and relationships take a hit.

Older woman, many younger women in our lives are tired, frustrated, and feel alone in their efforts, as if no one cares about the sacrifices they are making. Their relationships at home and elsewhere are frayed. We are called to model kindness for them and to train these young women to develop a kind heart and walk.

Younger woman, this quality is essential to learn if you want to honor the Lord. It flows out of a *sophron* mind and a heart that is fixed on Christ, and it makes all the difference in the world—both in your personal well-being and in the atmosphere you create around you.

If we wish to progress together toward the Titus 2 model for women, if we want to adorn the doctrine and gospel of Christ and His beauty to the world, we need a different kind of heart.

A *kind* kind of heart.

GIFTS IN KIND

On the surface, a study on kindness could seem insignificant compared to weightier subjects. It's easy to underestimate and overlook the importance of this quality. But I assure you that kindness is no trifling notion in the Christian vocabulary. I believe Paul intended it to matter as much to us as all the other essentials of the Titus 2 curriculum for women.

That's because a woman's spirit and tone has the ability to determine the climate around her, whether at home, at work, at the gym, or at church. And this makes kindness indispensable—in our relationships with others and for our gospel witness in the world. When we submit to Christ's lordship and serve others with humility and kindness, our words and actions can have a greater impact on those around us than a hundred sermons and orchestrated church outreaches. But when we don't, when we give in to unsound thinking and unkind attitudes, everyone suffers.

Let's be intentional about pursuing KINDNESS.

So with the same concern we feel for being pure and self-controlled, for avoiding slander and sins of the tongue, let's also be intentional about pursuing kindness—because it is every bit as important as the others.

GOOD AND KIND

The Greek word translated "kind" in Titus 2:5—*agathos*—is rendered as "good" almost every other time it appears in the New Testament. Sometimes it is used as an adjective to describe another word, as in "good works" or "good deeds." Various Bible scholars and commentators define this word as meaning "good and benevolent, profitable, useful,"[2] "beneficial in its effect,"[3] and "kind, helpful, and charitable."[4]

What Paul is exhorting here, in other words, is more than simply a nice, friendly feeling. *Agathos* is kindness that goes somewhere. It's a benevolent disposition coming to life, turning into active goodness.

The kindness inside us, in other words, becomes the goodness that others receive from us. It's a process that starts inside and inevitably moves outward. It's not just wanting to be kind or having kind thoughts and feelings, but being kind.

Author Jerry Bridges reminds us that this kind of kindness and goodness is rooted in humility and others-centeredness—no small challenge, as our natural bent is just the opposite:

> Apart from God's grace, most of us naturally tend to be concerned about our responsibilities, our problems, our plans. But the person who has grown in the grace of kindness has expanded his thinking outside of himself and his interests and has developed a genuine interest in the happiness and well-being of those around him.[5]

Am I a kind woman? In heart attitudes as well as outward actions? This is a question that pierces us when God's Word holds up a mirror in our family rooms and kitchens and hallways, our cars and minivans and workplaces. At times, instead of kindness and goodness, what we see reflected back is harshness and criticism. Barking and berating. Touchiness and irritability.

We may try to justify ourselves. After all, aren't we the ones who make sure everybody gets their meals and has their clothes washed?

Yes.

Will we leave the office early tonight and leave everyone to do our work for us? No.

Will we fail to show up when we're scheduled to help out at church?

Of course not.

Will we come around later, if necessary, to apologize if we reacted sharply toward someone earlier in the day?

Maybe—although we may be tempted to point out the circumstances that provoked us.

The people in our lives know they can count on us to be there when they need us. And if our spirit isn't always kind while we do our serving, is that really such a big deal? Shouldn't they just be thankful for all we do for them?

So we go through our days, checking off items from our to-do lists. We perform the duties others demand or expect of us. But are we doing it with a kind heart?

And if not, then what good are we really doing, and how are our relationships being affected?

CHANNELS OF BLESSING

I love the New Testament account of a follower of Christ most commonly known as Dorcas (the Greek equivalent of her Hebrew name Tabitha). The book of Acts tells us that she "was full of good [*agathos*] works and acts of charity" (9:36).

Here was a woman whose relationship with Christ moved her to pour out her life in practical acts of kindness toward those in need. Her life was a picture of true kindness in action. And the phrase "full of " ["abounding with"—NASB] implies that her charitable acts were not performed as begrudging service or out of a mere sense of duty. That became even more clear when tragedy struck, and the life of this generous-hearted woman was snuffed out:

> In those days she became ill and died, and when they had washed her, they laid her in an upper room. Since Lydda was near Joppa, the disciples, hearing that Peter was there, sent two men to him, urging him, "Please come to us without delay." So Peter rose and went with them. And when he arrived, they took him to the upper room. All the widows stood beside him weeping and showing tunics and other garments that Dorcas made while she was with them. (vv. 37–39)

This poignant description of the widows she had blessed, grieving next to her lifeless body, suggests that Dorcas genuinely cared for the people she served with her acts of kindness. They didn't just miss what she had done for them. They missed *her*.

Who will weep at your funeral as they think about your kind heart and the ways you have served and blessed them and demonstrated the kindness of Christ to them?

And how will you be remembered by your family, your closest friends, and others who knew you? Will they remember only what you did for them, or will there be a lingering fragrance because of how you did it?

Will they remember both the sacrifices you made *and* the smile they could always count on to warm their day?

Will they remember the extra time you took *and* the way you put your arms around them at the end of the day and told them how much you loved them?

Will they just remember the chugging sound of the washing machine running while they were drifting off to sleep, or will they also recall the soft sound of your voice humming a tune while waiting for the last load to dry?

Will they remember you as both a hard worker *and* an instrument of grace and goodness?

It's not clear what Dorcas' friends expected Peter to do when they called for him to come after the beloved benefactress died. But what happened next quickly got the attention of the whole town:

> Peter put them all outside, and knelt down and prayed; and turning to the body he said, "Tabitha, arise." And she opened her eyes, and when she saw Peter she sat up. And he gave her his hand and raised her up. Then, calling the saints and widows, he presented her alive. And

> it became known throughout all Joppa, and
> many believed in the Lord. (vv. 40–42)

All that time and effort spent making clothing for widows who had no other means of support had spelled L-O-V-E. And such kindness stood in stark contrast to the unbelieving world, where widows were often left to fend for themselves and faced probable destitution. Dorcas' life shone a spotlight on the love of Christ. It endeared her to those who had witnessed and been touched by her kindness. The power and beauty of her life moved them to call for the apostle when she died. And as a result of her being raised back to life, "many" put their faith in Him.

And that's the ripple effect of Christian kindness and the impact it can have on our witness in the world.

Kindness—true goodness—sometimes shows itself in tireless effort and sleepless nights. It can translate into grocery shopping for the family instead of shoe shopping for ourselves. It can mean relinquishing our plans for the afternoon when a daughter really needs to talk or hosting neighbors on a Friday night instead of enjoying a quiet evening to ourselves.

But the goal of it all is to show others the goodness of Christ—on a practical, personal, you-matter-to-me basis. And to do that consistently and well, we all need the training, accountability, and support Titus 2 relationships can provide. Older women need to model *agathos* for younger women and teach them the value of kindness. And younger women need to learn from older women that *people* matter more than any other *tasks* you might accomplish.

And, yes, people can be perturbing. Marriage and family life would be a lot less stressful if husbands and children didn't some-times act irresponsibly or disregard our feelings or instructions. Ministry would go more smoothly and be less demanding if people weren't so needy or would just get their act together. Many of the issues we face in our jobs would go away if it weren't for inexperienced coworkers, demanding clients, or impatient customers.

> When we serve people, we SERVE CHRIST.

When we serve people, we serve Christ. Yes, people may cause the lion's share of our headaches. But when we serve people, we serve Christ. And when we treat people with kindness rather than indifference or impatience, we become channels of blessing, dispensing gracious words and actions that can't help but adorn the gospel of Christ.

KINDNESS BEGINS AT HOME

The woman whose description we know so well from Proverbs 31 is another lovely, biblical model of kindness in action. Wherever this strong, gifted, diligent woman goes, she leaves a trail of goodness, and she ministers grace to everyone around her:

> She opens her mouth with wisdom,
>> and the teaching of kindness
>> is on her tongue. (v. 26)

But note who benefits first from this woman's industry and goodwill. For her, kindness begins at home. With her family. With her inner circle. With those who share her daily life. Her kindness toward her husband, for example, is displayed in a daily commitment that remains undiminished with the passing of time or when their relationship may be in a hard place:

> She does him good, and not harm,
>> *all the days of her life.* (v. 12)

Not a day is wasted by lashing out in frustration and anger or being passive-aggressive. Every day is seen as an opportunity to do her husband good with her attitude, words, and actions. This is a huge gift she gives to him—and to herself, as her husband responds with the highest of praise for his wife.

The Proverbs 31 woman's selfless, thoughtful deeds also bless her entire family as she labors tirelessly and faithfully to ensure their needs are met.

> She is not afraid of snow for her household,
>> for all her household are clothed in scarlet....

> She looks well to the ways of her household
> > and does not eat the bread of idleness.
> > Her children rise up and call her blessed...
> (vv. 21, 27–28)

The fact is, nowhere am I more tempted to be selfish and lazy than in my home and my closest relationships. And I fear this is true for most of us—wives and moms, as well as those who live with other family members or friends. Too often, I'm afraid, we show more concern and kindness for neighbors, colleagues, store clerks, or complete strangers than for those who live under the same roof with us or who are related to us by blood or marriage.

If a couple were staying at our house for the weekend, we'd be sure clean towels were in the bathroom, their linens were freshly washed, dinner was flexible to their schedule, and a fresh pot of coffee was brewing in the morning. But when our own kids and husband need something—well, they know where the refrigerator is and how to turn on the oven.

Right?

Managing a busy household, dealing with the daily tasks related to serving husbands and kids—or whatever other responsibilities you may have—requires diligence and discipline day in and day out. It requires hard work, sometimes exhausting work. But it also requires kindness—or as one commentator put it: "a lack of irritability in light of the nagging demands of mundane and routine household duties."[6]

And that's where things can get challenging. It's so easy for us to be like the woman who once lamented to me with refreshing candor, "I'm only good enough to look good to the world." At home, it's often another story.

When I'm out speaking at a conference, I can be exceedingly gracious, kind, and patient with long lines of women who want to share their burdens and their (at times long, detailed) stories, looking them in the eyes, never complaining about my tired, aching back and feet. But when those closest to me—in my home, my family, or our ministry—need a listening ear, an attentive heart, or a thoughtful act, I can be preoccupied, unfeeling, or just too busy.

> Nowhere am I more tempted to be selfish and lazy than in my home and my CLOSEST relationships.
>
> Too often, we show more concern and kindness for complete STRANGERS than for those who live under the same roof with us.

Who among us hasn't had the experience of being in the middle of a tense, unkind exchange at home, only to instantly change our tone and talk warmly with an outsider who calls or stops by? What does that say to our loved ones about how we value them and about the authenticity of our "kindness" to others?

Yes, kindness at home takes extra effort. Home is where we experience most acutely those daily annoyances and disappointments that tempt us to develop an attitude. So kindness at home also requires extra helpings of grace, which in turn requires daily dependence on God and the support of our Titus 2 sisters.

Already, in the short time I've been a wife, I've witnessed at moments the distance-creating, intimacy-killing impact of a lack of kindness on my part toward my husband. Unkind words spoken thoughtlessly, kind words left unspoken, inconsiderate actions; being too self-absorbed to notice and celebrate an accomplishment in my husband's business; wounding him in sensitive areas with insensitive teasing; being too busy with my own stuff to carry out small acts of kindness that would serve and bless him.

But I've also experienced the incredible importance and power of kindness in a marriage. I have seen it modeled in the marriages of some of my closest friends and of my Titus 2 mentors. And Robert's tender heart and his consistent kindness—always looking for ways to serve and bless me—have inspired me to be more tuned in to how I can do good to him. Being the recipient of his kindness has increased my desire to outdo him in this area.

Often, I've found, it's the little things—the simple expressions of gratitude and kindness—that express love to my husband and set the tone in our relationship. Leaving encouraging sticky notes in his OneYear Bible when he is headed out on a trip. Turning down the sheet on his side of the bed at night. Delivering a sandwich and cold root beer on a hot day when he's outside working on a project. Stopping in the middle of a busy work day to head downstairs to his study and find out how his day is going. Honoring his preferences over mine. Assuming the best when he forgets to tell me a piece of news. Choosing to overlook some perceived (or real) slight rather than grinding his nose in it. A kind heart expressed in kind words and kind deeds oils our relationship and softens and draws our hearts toward each other.

Your call to kindness at home will probably take different forms from mine. It may involve curbing a sharp reaction to a childish accident, replenishing the fridge with snacks for a teen, helping a roommate with a project, repeating yourself gently to an elderly parent. But if we were all to demonstrate true kindness toward the people who know us best and see us at our worst, our more public displays of affection would likely ring more true. And I suspect that if we showed more kindness at home, we'd also find ourselves growing genuinely kinder toward everyone else.

Kindness needs to start at home and in our closest relationships. But it doesn't need to *stay* there. As we train each other and let ourselves be trained in kindness, here are some of the other places where our goodness could—and should—be evident.

The family of God

"As we have opportunity," the Bible says, "let us do good to everyone, and especially to those who are of the household of faith" (Gal. 6:10).

Especially to those.

Many people view "church" as primarily a place to show up once a week and invest an hour of time into their spiritual savings account. But that's not what church is supposed to be! Jesus intended His church to be a family—a "household." Not a place, but a people who live out the gospel daily; redeemed men and women who gather together regularly for worship, encouragement, instruction, and service. And the many opportunities for kindness that exist within these relationships—woman to woman, friend to friend, older to younger, younger to older, family to family—can provide a rich source of blessing that builds each other up and keeps each other going.

The roots of this kind of mutual care and consideration among God's people can be traced back to the

Old Testament, where the law prescribed, for example, that if you saw an ox or a sheep wandering astray, you weren't allowed to just ignore it. If you knew the person it belonged to, you were to walk it back to its owner. If you weren't sure whose it was or if the journey was more than you could manage, you were to take the animal home with you and keep it safe until the owner came looking for it (see Deut. 22:1–4).

That's the kind of loyalty and kindness that is meant to mark our relationships with fellow members of Christ's body. For as 1 John 4:20 tells us, "he who does not love his brother whom he has seen cannot love God whom he has not seen." And when we open our hearts in generous love and a spirit of kindness toward our fellow believers, we testify to the kindness we've received from God.

So as you encounter fellow believers at church, at Bible study, as they come to mind through the week, or even as you interact online, consider how you might be able to extend kindness that goes deeper than shallow "Hi, how's it going?" hallway conversations. Because most people aren't doing "fine, thanks." And your gift of timely kindness—asking sincere questions, expressing interest in the happenings in their life, offering practical assistance for a need they're facing, or stopping to pray together—may be the means by which God ministers grace to them that day.

The poor and needy

Throughout the Scripture we see God's heart for the underserved and the overlooked, the weak and the disenfranchised. The noble woman of Proverbs 31 expresses that heart as she

> opens her hand to the poor
> and reaches out her hands to the needy. (v. 20)

No, it's not our responsibility to solve everyone's problems, to feel as if the weight of people's suffering is ours alone to bear. But God does call each of us to be sensitive toward the plight of those He brings to our attention. And He calls us to demonstrate His kindness to them in practical, need-meeting ways.

And who better than those who have been on the receiving end of God's amazing kindness to be on the lookout for people who are in need of His grace—especially those who may not be expecting anyone's help.

Reaching out in kindness can be as simple as choosing to "see" a person panhandling on the street instead of looking the other way—looking that person in the eye and offering a little something without judging how they will spend it. It can involve asking a widow to sit with us at church, helping out at a food pantry, offering to take a senior in the neighborhood to doctor appointments. But as God leads and as we follow, the borders of our kindness may eventually reach far beyond our natural comfort zone or our normal circle of relationships.

I've watched in awe, for instance, as many of my friends have opened their hearts and homes to care for "the least of these"—orphans, abused or neglected children, special needs children—through foster care, providing "safe homes," and adoption. What a beautiful way to put on display the heart of our heavenly Father who opened His heart and home to bring us into His family when we had nothing to offer Him except our poverty, dysfunction, sin, and need.

In recent years, I have received much joy through occasional involvement at a women's prison where God is at work in an unusual way. The opportunity to offer the kindness of Christ to damaged, broken women who are incarcerated on drug charges or as sex offenders, even some who are serving life sentences for first-degree murder, has reminded me that grace grows best in hard places. It has opened my heart to experience deeper streams of His kindness and blessing, often through the very women I am reaching out to.

Our enemies

And now for the most radical sphere of all—showing kindness to enemies. Responding with gentleness and goodness to those who dislike or even hate us. Doing good for those who would do us harm. Actively seeking the good of those we have reason to fear. That's a prospect that can tie our stomach in knots.

But if it weren't for Christ Himself showing kindness to us, not one of us would have a single blessing to our name. We would simply be God's sworn, forever enemies, with no hope on our part of anything except His righteous wrath and just judgment. Paul says as much in the third chapter of Titus:

> If it weren't for Christ showing kindness to us, NOT ONE OF US would have a single blessing to our name.

> For we ourselves were once foolish,
> disobedient, led astray, slaves to various
> passions and pleasures, passing our days in
> malice and envy, hated by others and hating
> one another. (v. 3)

That's a description of you and me before Jesus saved us. Even for those of us who came to know Him as young children, at our core, we were disobedient, malicious, and hateful. So how did God treat us? Here's how:

> But when the goodness and loving kindness
> of God our Savior appeared, he saved us, not
> because of works done by us in righteousness,
> but according to his own mercy ... (vv. 4–5)

His goodness and kindness toward us were not based on how we treated Him or on any worthiness in us. Likewise, the kindness we are to show to others is not conditional on their behavior or acceptability. Rather, it's an expression of the kindness we have received from Christ, flowing through us to others.

Even to our enemies.

"I don't have any enemies," you may say. But think again. We're not necessarily talking about super-villains here. Your enemies could simply be people with whom you seem to be at odds. Think about who annoys you or resents you, who often hurts or angers you, who you tend to approach warily if at all. They may be among your family or within your church or from your past. They may live near you, necessitating all-too-frequent contact. Or you may be distanced from them, preferring never to see them again if you can help it.

But consider: what might the kindness of God be leading you to do if your heart was like His heart? And what might it look like if your response toward these people reflected the blessing Christ poured out on you when you were still His enemy?

To be kind is to be like God. And when we are kind to those who are undeserving and unkind to us, we show them the amazing, undeserved kindness of God.

CHRIST-CENTERED KINDNESS

"Be kind to one another," writes Paul in Ephesians 4:32.

"Teach what is good, and so train the young women … to be … kind," he adds in Titus 2:3–5.

Agathos—kindness of heart, kindness in action—is an indispensable part of the Titus 2 curriculum for both older and younger women.

Such kindness can be costly—costly to our time, our plans, our comfort, our privacy. But when we exercise it in Jesus' name, kindness can provide us with some of our best opportunities to do what we've been put on this earth to do—to bring glory to God and make known the life-giving, transforming gospel of Christ.

> Our KINDNESS may be the window through which those around us are enabled to see HIS BEAUTY.

Our kindness may be the window through which those around us are enabled to see His beauty. Because kind women—younger and older together—paint an exquisite picture of the gospel. Our lives put on display "the riches of [God's] kindness"—the kindness that "is meant to lead [us] to repentance" (Rom. 2:4). The kindness that can bring about true transformation in those who experience it through us.

The kindness that adorns both us and the gospel we proclaim.

MAKING IT PERSONAL

Older women

1. Dorcas showed the kindness of Christ by helping the poor and needy around her. How might you use your skills to show kindness? How might you mentor or encourage a younger woman in the process?

_____

_____

_____

_____

_____

2. Many younger women feel tired and overwhelmed and can become frustrated when their service and sacrifices appear to go unnoticed. What did you learn in that season that could be helpful to share with a younger woman who is struggling?

_____

_____

_____

_____

3. How could you reach out in kindness to a younger woman in a way that would encourage her and help lift her load?

_____

_____

_____

_____

_____

_____

Younger women

1. Who comes to mind when you think of a Dorcas—a woman who loves Jesus and is a model of kindness and ministering to people's practical needs? What can you learn from her example?

_____

_____

_____

_____

_____

2. Would the people who live in your home and work with you consider you a kind woman? Why or why not?

_____

_____

_____

_____

_____

_____

3. When we get stretched and overly busy with tasks, it's easier to be cranky than kind (think of Martha). How could meditating on the kindness of Christ be an encouragement and motivation to show kindness when you're in that place?

_____

_____

_____

_____

_____

_____

100 DIFFERENT
KINDS OF KINDNESS

Practical, Thoughtful Ways to Be an Instrument of Grace in the Lives of Others

It's time to put into practice what you've learned. The *Revive Our Hearts* Team has put together this list of ideas to give you a jump start on your way to living a life of deep and active kindness. We've left some room for you to add your own ideas to each category.

Be an instrument of grace to . . .

Your Family

1. Greet your family members when they get up in the morning or come in the door. Say goodnight before you (or they) crawl into bed.

2. Have your spouse or roommate's tea/coffee ready for them when they first come into the kitchen in the morning.

3. Without complaining, pick up the socks your kids left on the floor.

4. Make a special meal or snack for those you live with "just because."

5. Ask a family member about their day, and listen with your full attention.

6. When a family member asks you to do something that they enjoy but isn't necessarily your favorite, do it with them anyway. Ask them questions and find out what it is they really like about that activity.

7. Do another household member's least favorite chore without being asked.

8. Leave a sticky note with a message of love somewhere a family member will be sure to see it: in their lunchbox, in their Bible, or on the bedroom door.

9. Take a cue from Nancy and deliver a cold root beer to family members doing yard work.

10. Write letters to your children on their birthdays expressing the qualities you appreciate about them. Let them know how much you love being their mother.

11. Watch a family member's favorite movie, television show, sports team, or YouTube channel with them—no matter how painful it is!

12. Write your children a note when you "catch" them doing something good. Help them to see that you notice.

13. Be spontaneous: drop everything and go to the beach, on a picnic, to the mall, or even on a mini-vacation with little to no warning.

14. Be mindful of special dietary needs. Is a family member counting calories? Grab some healthy options from the store. Finals week for the students in your life? Stock up on late-night study snacks.

15. Ask a family member if he or she needs any clothes ironed or if you can wash, dry, and put away a load of their laundry.

16. Vacuum your spouse's vehicle and take it to the car wash (or better yet, wash and wax by hand!).

17. The next time a family member wants to tell you a story, put your phone down, look him or her in the eye, and ask follow-up questions to show that you're engaged.

18. Give up your favorite chair during family movie night, and sit in the spot that nobody likes.

19. Take the trash to the curb when it's not your "job." Collect the bins and put them away when it's done.

20. If you normally don't initiate physical contact, make a point of giving a hug, offering an arm, or just being physically available to family members who are more "touchy."

Add Your Own Ideas

_____

_____

_____

_____

_____

Be kind to one another, tenderhearted, forgiving one another,
as God in Christ forgave you.
—Ephesians 4:32

Your Friends

21. Send a handwritten note to a friend you've felt out of touch with.

22. Is your friend in a busy season? Tell her you'd like to provide one meal per week for her family for a month. Then cook (or order) away!

23. Call or text just to tell your friend how much you appreciate her. Be specific in saying how she encourages and inspires you.

24. Ask your friend how you can pray for her, and stop and pray at that moment. Then follow up at a later time with an applicable verse and ask how things are going.

25. Drop off a friend's favorite coffee drink at her office or home. The 3 p.m. struggle is real!

26. Does your friend have a new baby? Offer to take a night shift or care for the baby for an afternoon so mom can nap.

27. Make spring cleaning a group project. Wash a friend's windows, walls, or offer to help deep clean a room in her home.

28. Be the chauffeur for a friend's kids' activities for a weekend. Let the kids eat in your car, and don't complain about the crumbs.

29. Be the initiator—don't wait for her to call you for coffee or lunch. Beat her to the punch!

30. Pick up a friend's grocery order, deliver it to her home, and help her put it away.

31. Help a friend with holiday prep: wrap presents, bake cookies, decorate the house, or even shop for her.

32. If you're not from the same area, take an interest in where your friend grew up. Visit it with her if you have the opportunity! Get to know her people.

33. Think of the last time your friend offended or sinned against you. Determine to let love cover that offense right now, forgive her, and never bring it up again.

34. Is your friend feeling blue? Bake a batch of chocolate chip cookies and deliver them—the warmer, the better!

35. If you go shopping together, make a mental inventory of the things your friend admires. Go back and purchase an item or two to give as a birthday or Christmas gift or even just a fun surprise.

36. Be the friend who asks how you can pray for her. Every. Single. Week.

37. That necklace, scarf, or bracelet she always compliments you on? Tell her you want her to have it.

38. Buy concert tickets to her favorite musical group or plan a special activity for the two of you. Try to think about what your friend would truly enjoy, not just the things you "always" do together. Arrange childcare for her children if necessary.

39. Help her navigate relational conflict by being a good listener. Avoid being a "fixer," but do provide encouragement from Scripture.

40. Acknowledge a friend's pain on difficult days: holidays after the loss of a loved one, anniversaries of traumatic events, birthdays of deceased family members, dates of miscarriages. Send a card or flowers, drop off coffee or chocolate, allow space for grief.

Add Your Own Ideas

_____

_____

_____

_____

> *Love one another with brotherly affection.*
> *Outdo one another in showing honor.*
> *—Romans 12:10*

Your Neighbors and Beyond

41. Welcome new neighbors to your apartment building or neighborhood with a home-cooked meal or a gift card for pizza. Make sure to give them your phone number in case they need a hand—or just a friend.

42. Host a simple "block party" in your yard. Provide hot dogs, lemonade, and an opportunity to get to know your neighbors.

43. Offer to water a neighbor's garden or collect their mail when they go on vacation.

44. Tie a balloon on a neighbor's front door with a note of encouragement and verse.

45. At the beginning of planting season in your area, give each person on the block a four-pack of annuals to plant with an encouraging note and Scripture verse.

46. Host a backyard Bible club or other children's activity. Keep it outdoors and invite parents to attend for safety.

47. Keep a small amount of cash on hand so when your neighbor kids come around selling items for fundraisers, you can cheerfully participate.

48. Be the neighbor that says "Hello" first. Engage your neighbors in conversation, then jot down a note so you can remember the details they tell you.

49. Offer to run errands for elderly neighbors or drive them to doctor's appointments, the grocery store, or the pharmacy.

50. Create a "community garden" in your front yard. Plant a selection of veggies in sight of the road or sidewalk, and make signs letting your neighbors know they're free for the taking.

51. Do a neighborhood prayer walk. With other families or just your own, walk around your neighborhood praying for the families that live in each home. If they ask what you're doing, ask them how you can pray!

52. Leave gift certificates to local businesses with an "anonymous act of kindness" note on their door.

53. Offer to help a single parent in your area with school drop-off or pick-up.

54. Volunteer at a school in your community (public and/or Christian), even if you don't have children who go there.

55. When eating out, choose a young family and tell the server you'd like to pay for their meal.

56. Study what your coworkers like to drink, and on the next rainy day, go for a coffee/tea/soda run. Write a special note of thanks or a verse of Scripture on their disposable drink cup.

57. Keep a few five or ten dollar gift cards to fast food restaurants in your wallet. At the bank or the grocery store, give one (along with a smile!) to a clerk who seems ready for a break.

58. In the store parking lot, offer to return the cart of an older person or a parent with small children.

59. Choose a public safety agency and deliver care packages containing snacks, gift cards to local businesses, bottled water, and a note thanking them for their service.

60. When visiting the doctor or flying on an airplane, keep a copy of a Christian book on suffering in

your purse, diaper bag, or briefcase. Be deliberate about engaging those around you in conversation. When an opening arises (and it will), use the opportunity to share the book.

Add Your Own Ideas

_____

_____

_____

_____

_____

"In the same way, let your light shine before others,
so that they may see your good works
and give glory to your Father who is in heaven."
—Matthew 5:16

Your Church

61. Arrange a free childcare opportunity for parents on Valentine's Day, during the busy Christmas season (so they can go shopping together), or anytime to provide a night out.

62. Be an example of someone who doesn't complain about your church or dwell on the negative.

63. Send care packages to college students in the middle of a semester.

64. Sit with a parent who is alone in church with his or her children to help with young ones.

65. Invite those without local family to your home for a holiday meal.

66. Invite a single person to sit with your family at church—or go and sit with him or her.

67. Send a special card to widows and widowers at Christmastime acknowledging their feelings of loss and reminding them of God's goodness.

68. Offer to pay for a young family's child/children to attend church camp or a youth trip.

69. Host a game night for your church's teens in your home.

70. Organize a group to do yard work for elderly or disabled members.

71. Invite moms with young children to meet at the park. Provide snacks for the moms and the kids.

72. When you read a great Christian book, order an extra copy to give away.

73. Set up valet parking! Enlist the help of young men in your church to park and retrieve vehicles on bad weather days.

74. Visit a shut-in and listen to a recording of the previous Sunday's message together. Read Scripture and pray for your church and each other.

75. Go Christmas caroling at the homes of those who could use encouragement around the holidays.

76. Offer your services for a skill you possess to those who can't afford to pay for help: cleaning, hairstyling, snowplowing, tree removal, home repair, auto repair, clothing alterations, etc.

77. Offer an empty room in your home to a single person, college student, or young married couple who needs housing.

78. Deliver a care package to families experiencing grief. Include snacks, Kleenex, bottled water, toiletries, a scented candle, a cozy blanket, and a journal or sketchbook.

79. Sit in the hospital waiting room with the loved ones of someone who is having surgery.

80. Gather a group of women to pray over each name in the church directory.

Add Your Own Ideas

_____

_____

_____

_____

_____

*So then, as we have opportunity, let us do good to everyone,
and especially to those who are of the household of faith.*
—Galatians 6:10

*Ministers of the Gospel (pastors, pastors' wives, church
staff, missionaries, parachurch ministry staff,
Bible teachers, authors, podcasters, etc.)*

81. Have lunch or food for a morning break delivered
    to your church for the staff to enjoy.

82. Enlist multiple people to "text bomb" a staff
    member on the same day with a Scripture verse
    and sentence of gratitude for how God is using
    them to make a difference.

83. Send thank you notes to an entire church or min-
    istry staff, letting them know that their service is
    noticed and appreciated.

84. Give your pastor's wife a gift card for coffee, can-
    dles, lotion, etc.—something she might like but
    wouldn't normally buy for herself.

85. Send your church office staff flowers or other
    treats on Administrative Professionals Day.

86. If your pastor has young children, offer yourself on Sunday mornings to help his wife get the family up, fed, and dressed for church.

87. Volunteer at your local crisis pregnancy center. Carry business cards to give out to women you meet who need assistance.

88. Build up your pastor's children by talking to and encouraging them. It's tough being in the spotlight—not to mention being the focus of sermon illustrations!

89. Give children's ministry leaders and teachers a gift card to a department or craft store. You'd be surprised how many spend their own money on projects for the kids.

90. Have a book shower for a missionary family. Ask what books, Bible studies, and reference materials they need, collect the resources at church, and mail them off to the family.

91. Write your favorite podcaster a handwritten note expressing your appreciation for their commitment to the gospel.

92. Give church staff families access to your cabin, vacation home, or RV to enjoy a low-cost family getaway.

93. Send a note of thanks to your church musicians for their service and creativity. Consider including a gift of money to assist them in purchasing music or caring for their instrument.

94. Meet one-on-one with your pastor's wife and ask questions to really get to know her and understand where she is emotionally and spiritually. Jot down some questions in advance in case your conversation slows down.

95. Email a parachurch ministry and ask them for any staff prayer needs. Pray for their requests, and then send a note of encouragement to the people you prayed for.

96. If an administrative issue can wait until Monday, avoid talking to church staff or other about it on Sunday. Full-time ministry workers need a sabbath, too.

97. Speak kindly about your pastor to someone else every Sunday. Tell him you're praying for him— and do it!

98. Give your pastor's family a gift card to a clothing store before Christmas or Easter. They'll appreciate the chance to stock up on "Sunday best."

99. Offer to host a missionary family while on furlough. Give them their own space as much as possible. Love on their children and introduce them to the children in your neighborhood.

100. Pray for ministers of the gospel and their families by name. Pray with them, pray for them, storm the throne of grace on their behalf. Be the first line of defense when they come under attack.

Add Your Own Ideas

_____

_____

_____

_____

_____

We ask you, brothers, to respect those who labor among you
and are over you in the Lord and admonish you,
and to esteem them very highly in love
because of their work.
—1 Thessalonians 5:12–13

NOTES

Epigraph: Mary Beeke, *The Law of Kindness: Serving with Heart and Hands* (Grand Rapids: Reformation Heritage, 2007), 31. Quote adapted with permission from the author.

1. Scripture does not explicitly state that Martha was the eldest sibling in her family. But many commentators believe the text suggests that this was the case—also that the home belonged to her and that she was responsible for managing the household.

2. Spiros Zodhiates, ed., *The Complete Word Study Dictionary: New Testament*, rev. Reissue ed. (Chattanooga: AMG, 1993), 62.

3. W.E. Vine, *The Expanded Vine's Expository Dictionary of New Testament Words: A Special Edition* (Minneapolis: Bethany, 1984), 493.

4. Matthew Henry, *Commentary on the Whole Bible,* ed. Leslie F. Church (Grand Rapids: Zondervan, 1961), 1902.

5. Jerry Bridges, *The Practice of Godliness: Godliness Has Value for All Things,* rev. Ed. (Colorado Springs: NavPress, 2008), 189.

6. Thomas D. Lea and Hayne P. Griffin, *1, 2 Timothy, Titus,* vol. 34 of *The New American Commentary* (Nashville: B&H, 1992), 301.

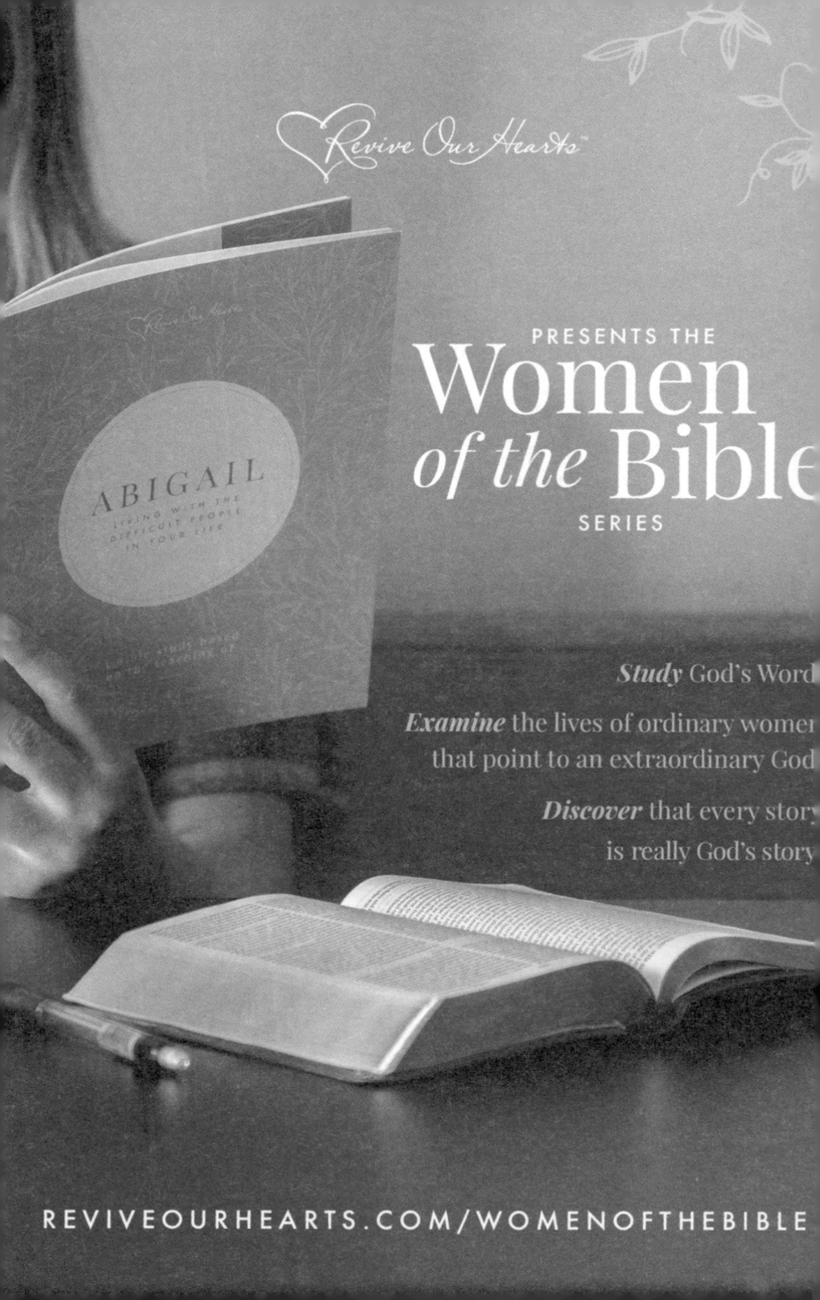
Revive Our Hearts
ABIGAIL
LIVING WITH THE DIFFICULT PEOPLE IN YOUR LIFE
PRESENTS THE
Women
of the Bibl
SERIES
Study God's Wor
Examine the lives of ordinary wome
that point to an extraordinary God
Discover that every stor
is really God's stor
REVIVEOURHEARTS.COM/WOMENOFTHEBIBLE